REIMAGINING

the

IGNATIAN

EXAMEN

Other Books by Mark E. Thibodeaux, SJ

*God's Voice Within: The Ignatian Way
to Discover God's Will*

*Armchair Mystic: Easing into
Contemplative Prayer*

*God, I Have Issues: 50 Ways to Pray No
Matter How You Feel*

REIMAGINING

the

IGNATIAN EXAMEN

Fresh Ways to Pray from Your Day

MARK E. THIBODEAUX, SJ

LOYOLA PRESS.
A JESUIT MINISTRY

Chicago

LOYOLA PRESS.
A JESUIT MINISTRY

3441 N. Ashland Avenue
Chicago, Illinois 60657
(800) 621-1008
www.loyolapress.com

Cover art credit: Markovka/Shutterstock.com

ISBN-13: 978-0-8294-4244-1
ISBN-10: 0-8294-4244-8
Library of Congress Control Number: 2014955633

Printed in the United States of America.

14 15 16 17 18 19 20 Versa 10 9 8 7 6 5 4 3 2 1

Contents

The Most Amazing Prayer You've Never Heard Of

One of the greatest mystics of all time, St. Ignatius of Loyola, believed that the prayer exercise called the "Examen" should be the *most important quarter-of-an-hour of a person's day*, and yet today most Christians have never even heard of it.

Why is the Examen so valuable?

St. Paul exhorts us to "pray without ceasing" (1 Thessalonians 5:17). I've learned that the closer I get to Christ, the more I really long to be with him always. It's not that I desire to be kneeling in a church or sitting in my comfy prayer-chair all day. I love the buzz of my life—the endeavor of human activity—too much to be sitting in contemplation all the time. No, what I long for is to have Christ join me in all the adventures and tedium of my active day. I love Christ so much that I want to share every minute of it with him.

My faith tells me that God is everywhere at all times, and that Christ is in my heart and embedded in all of creation—regardless of how conscious I am of his presence at any given moment. That's wonderfully consoling, but I want more! I want to *feel* his presence all the time. I want to feel him not only when I leave the nitty-gritty of my life and go to church; I want to feel his presence always! And I want to share with him even the smallest details of my life: the irritating e-mail I just received and the pleasant smile of the woman at the post office; the dread in my heart for the difficult meeting I'm about to step into and also the delight of biting into that perfectly sweet and crunchy apple during my break. I want to talk to Christ about the stupid thing I just said to my boss and also the little victory I had in getting that boring multiday task completed. Sure, I want to share with Christ the really big things: my grave sins and my overwhelming consolations, and I will share those big things during my daily meditation and when I go to Mass or confession. But the closer I grow to Christ, the more I want to share with him the seemingly insignificant things as well. I know that he's there, in the midst of it all, and I long to tap into his presence right there in the mud and muck, the pencils and French fries of my complicated yet incredibly ordinary life.

This is why the Examen is so awesome and powerful. It brings my nitty-gritty to God and God to my nitty-gritty.

I could go on and on about how wonderful the Examen is. I could tell you:

- how it unites me ever closer to God
- how it reveals God's perspective on my everyday life
- how it stirs me to give praise and thanksgiving for the countless gifts of God that have popped up in my day, and even to perceive the very presence of God in those gifts
- how it gives me an opportunity to recognize and apologize for my faults, and to grieve my failures and hurts and receive healing from them

- how it brings insight into what is really going on beneath the surface of my thoughts, words, and actions—into the very source of my motivations and machinations
- how it helps me discern how to handle the trickier aspects of my life, to know what interior gifts I need from God to do the right thing tomorrow, and to ask God for those gifts explicitly

I could provide pages of details about all these unbelievable benefits I receive from praying this brief prayer every day. But why waste another minute *reading* about the benefits when you can reap them for yourself? You'll know just what I'm talking about as soon as you try it.

What Is the Ignatian Examen?

Saint Ignatius of Loyola created the Examen to be a very short ("quarter of an hour") twice-daily prayer that can be prayed at any time that is most convenient. Most people enjoy praying the Examen during their lunch break and in the evening as they are winding down. At lunchtime, you look back at how your morning has gone and look forward to how your afternoon and evening might go. In the evening, you look back over your afternoon (since your lunchtime Examen) and look forward to how tomorrow morning might go. If you are new to the Examen, you may find it easier to start by praying it only once a day.[1]

---

1. For the sake of convenience, this book presumes that the reader is praying the Examen once a day at the end of the day. As you are reading through an Examen, you can make the adjustments necessary to fit your situation. For example, if you pray the Examen twice a day and are presently praying it at lunchtime, you will want to translate "look back at my day, today" as "look back at my morning" and to translate "I now look to tomorrow" as "I now look to this afternoon."

In the Examen, we review our recent past to find God and God's blessings in daily life. We also look back to find moments in the day when things didn't go so well—when we were hurt by something that happened to us, or when we sinned or made a mistake. We give praise and thanksgiving for the blessed moments. We ask forgiveness and healing for the difficult and painful moments. Having reflected on this past day, we then turn to the day yet to come and ask God to show us the potential challenges and opportunities of tomorrow. We try to anticipate which moments might go one way or the other for us: toward God's plan or away from it. We ask for insight into what graces we might need to live this next day well: patience, wisdom, fortitude, self-knowledge, peace, optimism. We ask God for that grace, and we trust that he wants us to succeed in our day even more than we do.

That's the basic idea behind the Ignatian Examen. Ignatius would say that this should be the most important moment of our day. Why? Because this moment affects every other moment.

Specifically, How Do You Do the Examen?

Ignatius provides a simple five-step routine for our daily Examen:

Give thanksgiving. I begin by giving God thanks for all the things I'm grateful for today. I allow my mind to wander as I reflect on the ways God has blessed me on this particular day. I allow big things and small things to arise—everything from the gift of my faith, to the gift of my marriage, to the easy commute to work today.

Ask for the Spirit. Next, I want to look at the moments in my day when I did not act so well. However, before doing so,

I ask God to fill me with his Spirit so that the Spirit can lead me through this difficult soul-searching. Otherwise, I'm liable to hide in denial, wallow in self-pity, or seethe in self-loathing.

Review and recognize failures. I look back at my day and ask the Lord to point out to me the moments when I have failed in big ways or small. I take a sobering look at the mistakes I've made this day.

Ask for forgiveness and healing. If I have sinned, I ask God to forgive me and set me straight again. If I have not sinned but simply made a mistake, I ask for healing of any harm that might have been done. I ask for help to get over it and move on. I also ask for wisdom to discern how I might better handle such tricky moments in the future.

Pray about the next day. I ask God to show me how tomorrow might go. I imagine the things I'll be doing, the people I'll see, and the decisions I'll be mulling over. I ask for help with any moments I foresee that might be difficult. I especially ask for help in moments when I might be tempted to fail in the way I did today.

To help me remember the five steps, I like to use a 5-Rs mnemonic:

- **Relish** the moments that went well and all of the gifts I have today.
- **Request** the Spirit to lead me through my review of the day.
- **Review** the day.
- **Repent** of any mistakes or failures.
- **Resolve,** in concrete ways, to live tomorrow well.

How Do You Use This Book?

There is no problem with simply sticking to the original five-step Examen as presented by St. Ignatius. But you may find that when you slightly change the reflection questions every day, the Examen will feel fresher and more spontaneous. The ultimate goal of all the Examens in this book is the same: to experience an encounter between God and the stuff of day-to-day life. But asking slightly *different* questions every day will yield slightly different results, and that will keep the experience dynamic and energizing.

One simple method: on the first day of the month, place your bookmark on Examen #1 and use that Examen to reflect upon your life. The next day, move to Examen #2, and so on. At the beginning of the next month, move the bookmark to #1 again and start all over. There are thirty-four Examens, so you can go through the month while skipping two or three that don't work as well for you.

If you don't care to, you don't need to be that regimented. Once you get to know the various Examens, you can skip around to match your moods and preferences. Or maybe you will find that certain Examens lend themselves easily to certain situations about which you are praying. Very well, go straight for those. All the Examens lead to the same place: a place of unity with God in the particulars of your life. Therefore, you can go to any Examen you like for any reason at all.

Some Tips before Getting Started

In the point in which I find what I am seeking, there I will rest, without anxiety to move forward until my heart is satisfied.
—St. Ignatius of Loyola, *The Spiritual Exercises*, #76

For many years, I have helped others learn and practice this prayer. So I know the pitfalls as well as the potential. Here are a few points to keep in mind.

Keep It Short

I strongly recommend that you keep your Examen under fifteen minutes. One of the unique qualities of this prayer is its nitty-gritty, on-the-spot, wash-and-wear, plug-and-play kind of spirit. The Examen isn't meant to be a deep and probing experience. It is designed to be a simple in-the-moment check-in that reminds me of God's presence and reorients me toward him.

Let's say I'm a commercial pilot in the middle of a long flight. I notice that engine two is running a little hot, as it has been doing of late. I know that this is not an imminently dangerous situation but that it will need to be readjusted by a mechanic later. When we arrive at our destination tonight, I'll let the ground crew know so that the night-shift mechanics can go "under the hood" and make a more permanent fix. In the meantime, I will simply keep an eye on it and make small adjustments from here in the cockpit.

How does this analogy apply to my spiritual life? The mechanic working under the hood for a permanent fix is my longer, deeper periods of contemplation and meditation, as well as other spiritual work, such as doing spiritual reading on the subject and speaking with my pastor, my spiritual director, or a friend with whom I share spiritual conversation. The Examen is analogous to the pilot checking the instruments from time to time and making small, in-flight adjustments to maximize the performance of the plane on a particular flight.

This is not to say that nothing big or important happens during the Examen. Sticking with the analogy, it is during in-flight check-ins that we discover most "under-the-hood" issues. But Examen time falls in the middle of the workday or at the end of a long, tiring day. So it is meant to be an on-the-spot, middle-of-it-all moment of prayer, not a sustained, thorough meditation.

One more logistical point: some people find that setting an alarm or timer for ten or fifteen minutes allows them to keep it short without having to check the time every few minutes. Setting an alarm allows one to get lost in the midst of prayer without having to worry about coming back to daily life in due time.

Skip to the Good Parts

On any given day, as I get started on a particular Examen in this book, I first read quickly over the entire thing, getting a feel for where it will take me. Then, as I begin to pray through the Examen, I linger and dwell on *only* the steps that really move me, that seem to be drawing fruit in me, and I move gently but quickly through the steps that don't seem to be grabbing me today. For example, Examen #18: "God, Others, Self" invites me to consider first my relationship with God, then my relationship with others, then my relationship with myself. There is no way that I can have meaningful reflection on these three distinct relationships in just fifteen minutes! So instead, I do a prayerful and very brief overview of these three relationships. In doing so, I may notice one of the three reflections really grabbed me—either because I was intrigued by an insight that popped up or because my heart was moved by a strong emotion as I reflected on that particular relationship. Well, I don't waste another minute on the other two relationships (maybe they'll be important next month, when I pray this Examen again). Instead, I go straight for the one that really grabbed me, spending the rest of the Examen on that one relationship and not giving another thought to the other two.

What is my point here? I shouldn't allow the eight or ten or twelve steps of a given Examen to weigh me down, forcing me to labor with each one until I come up with "an answer" before moving to the next step. This isn't a math problem! Instead, I let each step gently suggest where I might look in my heart for the one precise spot God wants to show me, like a parent helping a toddler look for Easter eggs in a meadow. "How about there? What about here?" Once I find that spot, I drop everything else and linger there with God for a while before moving on.

Sometimes, Break All the Rules

I've already suggested that you should feel free to skip over one step or another within a particular Examen. Now I go further:

there are times when you should feel free to pitch the whole thing! For example, as I write this, I'm still filled with gratitude for what happened to me last night. I was asked to drive to a nearby church to help two other priests hear confessions. I hesitated to say yes because I had something else to do that night that was important. But I felt the tug of my priestly calling and said yes. Well, I'm so glad I did because it was a beautiful and moving experience.

To anyone watching it would appear that nothing extraordinary happened. I listened to a group of teenaged confirmation candidates make their confessions. I chatted a bit with the other two priests before and afterward. I took the opportunity to go to confession myself. None of these events was very dramatic. But wow, I was so moved by the sincerity of those kids! And praying through the sacrament with each one of them, sharing in the suffering and pain of their difficult moments, proclaiming the words of absolution over their heads—the whole experience left me feeling the divine power of God's mercy that surged through my priestly hands and into their souls. And to close with the simple camaraderie of my brother priests and with the simple, unremarkable confession of my own sins—well, it was a night charged with the electricity of divinity. I came home "filled up" with God.

Before going to bed last night, I pulled out my collection of Examens and turned to the one that was next on my list, Examen #25: "Thank You for . . . Forgive Me for . . . Help Me with . . ." As I began to pray, the structure and steps felt too small and limited. The vessel of this Examen could not contain the overwhelming joy and gratitude I felt in my heart. So I pitched the whole thing and spent the entire Examen time thanking and praising God for my priesthood, for the goodness of these kids and these priests, and for the unfailing mercy of God. I just sat there in praise and thanksgiving.

Many times I approach my Examen overflowing with joy, gratitude, relief, or wonder. Other times I am filled not with joyful emotions but with negative ones. I've begun some Examens with great sadness, anger, shame, or confusion. When I enter the Examen filled with strong emotions from an experience I've just had or over the anticipation of something big about to happen, I often bypass the step-by-step format and sit with the Lord, expressing whatever strong emotions I feel at the moment and trying to get a sense of God's response back to me.

Don't Get Stuck on Sin

Unfortunately, the Ignatian Examen is often confused with the Examination of Conscience. They are similar in that they both lead a person through a review of his or her life. But these two prayer experiences have different goals.

The Examination of Conscience prepares you to confess your sins and ask for forgiveness. You spend all your prayer time looking at your sinful actions in the past.

The goal of the Ignatian Examen includes a reflection on sin and forgiveness, but it is much broader. The objective is to explore with God *all* the facets of my past, present, and future life, not just the bad parts in the past. God and I look together with a *holistic* view of my life: my sins and my virtues, my failures and successes, the things I'm grateful for and the things that drive me crazy, the future happenings I'm joyful about and the ones I dread as well, the peaks and the valleys, the nightmares and the sweet dreams—everything!

Reflecting on my sinfulness is one of the greatest gifts of the Ignatian Examen. Not only does it lead to my own experience of liberation, but it also tells me what specifically I need to work on to be a more effective follower of Jesus. However, I must be careful never to get stuck in guilt, sin, and failure. The essence of sin is selfishness. But dealing with my sins—reflecting on them, grieving over them, repenting of them—is still a focus on *me*. I'm still preoccupied with myself and have not yet become selfless and other-centered. So, *we spend time on our failures to move on from them, to turn those stumbling blocks into stepping-stones.*

In the Ignatian Examen, I explore my sins and allow God to forgive and heal me. I also spend time in thanksgiving, in dreaming great and holy dreams about my future, and in working out with God in specific terms how to make that divinely inspired future come to life.

Experiment with Tweet-Sized Journaling

I have found journaling to be a marvelous help in my experience of the Examen. But here's the catch: I never write more than a word, a phrase, or—at most—a tiny paragraph. My entry on any given day is never more than twenty words or so, and often it is only one or two.

Why does this work so well? These "tweet"-sized journal entries help me in at least three important ways. First, knowing that I need to put something down on paper by the end of the Examen keeps me sharply focused on the topic of my prayer.

It keeps my mind from wandering too far off point. Second, writing down some painful or previously unacknowledged truth brings it into the light and keeps me from denying it any longer. Sometimes my Examen helps me face a reality I've been denying for a while:

- "I'm really angry with ___."
- "I'm afraid of ___."
- "Hey, concerning ___, it's not as bad as I thought it was!"
- "I feel hurt about ___."

There are times when in the middle of my Examen such a thought will come to me. I write it down and then just look at what I've written for a moment. There's no denying it now. It's right there in black and white.

Finally, because I date each entry, I'm able to get a sense of where my heart has been lately. Before beginning my Examen, I sometimes glance back at the last couple of entries I've written. Doing so places me right back at the spot where I left off, or perhaps it will show me how far I've come in such a short time, how differently I feel today as opposed to the past few days. Every now and then, once a month or once a "season," I spend a whole Examen simply praying over my journal entries. Doing so can be a revelatory and moving experience.

Keep It Prayerful

Because the Examen is so concrete, it sometimes can drift away from being a prayer and become simply a thought exercise. If you were to perform this thought exercise every day—that is, if you daily spent a few minutes evaluating your day and assessing the good and bad points as well as assessing the challenges and opportunities that lie ahead—that would be a smart and fruitful investment of your time. Any introductory book on business administration will tell you the same. But for this ten-minute experience to be an Examen, it needs to be truly a time of prayer. And for it to be truly a prayer, *it needs to be God-centered.* In specific terms, this means:

- **I ask God to take the lead.** Rather than simply coming up with insights, I ask God to show me my day from his perspective. Derrick, a Jesuit friend of mine, told me once, "Sometimes, I say to God, 'Lord, you do the Examen of my day. I'll watch!' It goes to entirely different places when I let the Lord lead."

- **I talk to God instead of talking to myself.** Instead of saying to myself, "So tomorrow, I want to work on _____," I address God and say, "Lord, please help me work on _____ tomorrow."

- More than anything, **I *listen* for God's voice.** With my mind's eye, I *watch* for God. What is God trying to say to me right at this moment? What is God doing at this moment? Is he smiling at me? Holding my hand? Is he listening with loving concern? Does he have a word of advice? or warning? or affirmation? Is he silent and seemingly distant?

That last line about God perhaps being silent and seemingly distant is important because God often is silent, and when he is, it *feels as if* he were distant. Our faith tells us that God is never distant from us—that he dwells in every molecule of our being. But often we don't *feel* God's presence. That's OK! Don't worry about that. It is perfectly natural and normal, and every saint from Teresa of Avila to Theresa of Lisieux to Teresa of Calcutta has assured us of this. For it to be a prayer, then, we don't have to feel God's presence all the time; we simply have to be oriented toward God. We don't actually have to *hear* God speak, so long as we are *listening* in case he chooses to say something. It is the listening for God's voice that orients us toward him, whether or not he speaks on any given day.

Over Time, Develop Your Own Rituals for Beginning and Ending the Prayer

You will notice that every one of the Examens in this book begins with the first step of "I begin in my usual way" and ends with the last step of "I end in my usual way." I recommend that you slowly develop unique and personal rituals for beginning and ending your Examen. Some people begin the Examen with a recitation of a formulaic prayer such as the Our Father, with the singing of a simple song such as "Amazing Grace," or with the repetition of a favorite line from Scripture ("My heart is ready, O God. My heart is ready."). Others bow to their prayer spot as a way of declaring this a sacred space. Catholics usually begin with the sign of the cross. Many find it helpful to begin by taking some slow, deep breaths. All of these examples could also be rituals for ending one's Examen. The idea is to have a simple, short, prayerful way to enter this experience and a similarly helpful way to close it and get back to the day's tasks.

Here are basic templates to get you started until your own rituals evolve.

Template of a Beginning Ritual

- I make the sign of the cross.
- I say the Our Father or the Morning Offering.
- I sing or hum one verse or the refrain of my favorite hymn.
- I bow before my prayer spot.
- I place my hands, palms up, in a gesture of receptivity.
- I light a candle.
- I quiet myself down. I slow down my breathing. I sit very still for a moment and try to turn down the volume on my crazy, random thoughts and preoccupations.
- I ask God to make his presence known to me at this moment. I sense God's presence all around me and even within me. If it feels natural to do so, I allow myself to linger in this sense of God's presence. I descend into and soak in this experience for a moment, as though it were a hot bath. If I do not sense God's presence, I wait quietly and patiently for another moment. If I still do not sense God's presence, I don't let it bother me. I simply lean on my faith that he is here, even when I don't perceive his presence. I let my heart, mind, and soul remember what it does feel like when I do sense his presence, and I let that suffice for now.
- I then move on to the Examen of the day.

Template of a Closing Ritual

When I sense that it is time to close my Examen (perhaps my ten-minute timer has gone off), I ask myself if there are any last words I wish to say to the Lord. If I haven't yet made a statement about, a request for, or a promise regarding the future (the next day, the next week, etc.), I do so now. Then I close with one or two physical gestures.

- I place my hands together as a sign of closure.
- I blow out my candle.
- I sing or hum a closing verse or the refrain of my favorite hymn.
- I close with the Our Father or the Morning Offering.
- I make the sign of the cross.
- I bow before my prayer spot before leaving.

The Examens

Examen 1
Traditional Ignatian Examen

St. Ignatius himself recommends these five steps: Relish the good, Request the Spirit, Review the day, Repent from any wrongdoing, and Resolve to live well tomorrow.

1. I begin in my usual way.[2]

2. **First, I relish.** I ask God to reveal to me all the gifts and *graces* he has given me this day, from the really big ones (my life, safety, love) to the really small ones (a good night's sleep, an affirming phone call from a friend, a task completed, a compliment paid to me). For each gift that comes to mind, I spend a moment giving thanks and praise.

3. **Second, I request.** Knowing that I need God's help to see my darker side realistically but from the perspective of God's merciful love, I ask God to fill me with his Spirit. I ask God to be the leader and initiator of this prayer time, rather than letting me make it an obsessive brooding over the things I don't like about myself.

4. **Third, I review.** Going hour by hour, I review my day. In my imagination, I relive each significant moment of my day. I linger at the important moments, and I pass quickly through the less relevant ones.

---

2. For a template of a beginning ritual, see page xxii.

5. **Fourth, I repent.** As I review my day, I continue thanking God for all the gifts that I find in it. But now, I pause at any of the difficult moments of the day—when I had a bad thought, said something I shouldn't have, or did something inappropriate. I also pay attention to any missed opportunities, such as when I could have acted in a more Christian manner but didn't. When I find moments in which I was not fully the person I'm called to be, I stop and ask forgiveness from God. I try to sense his healing mercy washing over me, making me clean and whole.

6. **Fifth, I resolve.** With what I have learned during this prayer time about myself and my life, I ask God to show me, concretely, how he wants me to respond or what he wants me to do tomorrow. Perhaps more important, I ask God to show me what kind of person God is calling me to *be* tomorrow. I resolve to be that person. I might even make some sort of commitment to that effect. I ask God for the help to be the person I'm called to be.

7. I end in my usual way.[3]

---

3. For a template of a closing ritual, see page xxii.

Examen 2
Spiritual Freedom

We are *spiritually free* when our spiritual and emotional state of being is healthy. We are spiritually free when we are emotionally well-balanced and desirous of being a faithful, hopeful, and loving person. We are *spiritually unfree*[4] when our negative emotions and temptations have gotten the better of us, when we are too angry, sad, tempted, or scared to think straight. We are unfree when we are lethargic and not inspired to be more faithful, hopeful, and loving. We are unfree when we don't feel God's presence at this moment, and we either don't care or are too panicky to handle the situation well.

In this Examen you may explore the question, "What was my most unfree moment this morning?" By that we mean: When was I in a bad mood? When did the unfaithful, unhopeful, unloving side of me take over? When did I let my strong negative emotions control my thoughts and actions?

You may then explore the question, "What was my most free moment?" By that we mean: When was I in a really good mood? When did the most faithful, hopeful, and loving side of me run the show? When was I thinking clearly and objectively, thinking good and loving thoughts and making good and loving decisions?

---

4. For more on "spiritually free" and "spiritually unfree," see "Important Ignatian Terms," p. 81. Hereafter words in bold italic are referenced in that section.

1. I begin in my usual way.

2. I spend a few moments in gratitude, thanking God for one or two of the blessings, big and small, that I've received today: the good mood in which I woke up, a kind word from a friend, my undeserved good health, an easy commute to work, another day with my wonderful spouse.

3. Looking back, I ask God, "What was my most unfree moment today?" That is: At what moment was I being carried away by my own fears, resentments, cravings, addictions, anxieties, or despairing thoughts? In my imagination, I return to that specific moment in my day. I imagine God and myself watching this moment together, side by side. I imagine that we can look not only at the externals, as though watching a video from a hidden camera, but also that we can look at the internal movements. In other words, God and I watch as my heart fills to the brim with the negative emotion that swept me away.

4. I speak to God about what I see. I ask God for forgiveness or maybe for healing. I allow God to show me his perspective of the situation. Is there anything that I sense God is trying to tell me about this? I talk with him about this, especially acknowledging my deepest emotions about it.

5. Looking back again, I ask, "What was my most spiritually free moment today?" In which moment did I feel and act free from negativity, low and earthly thoughts and

emotions? At what point did I feel most *alive* and most in sync with God, even if I didn't notice it at the time?

6. Just as before, I imagine God and myself watching this grace-filled moment. We replay the moment here in my prayer time. We observe not only what happened, but also what was going on deep in my heart. I speak to God about this. I allow God to show me his perspective. We talk about it for a while. We celebrate that moment.

7. Now God and I look to tomorrow. How can I live my day tomorrow out of that freedom that I felt in today's grace-filled moment? What attitudes and behaviors will I adopt in order to avoid the pit of that unfree moment? What is God calling me to do to live in spiritual freedom?

8. I make whatever commitments I feel called to make. I ask God for help to keep that commitment.

9. I end in my usual way.

Naming the Grace

*I begin [my prayer] by asking God our Father for the grace that
I am seeking. Here it will be . . .*
—St. Ignatius of Loyola

The word **grace**[5] is used in many different ways. In this book we
are using it to mean "spiritual gift" or "virtue." I like to ask myself
the question, "If I could ask God for one spiritual gift right now
(courage, peace, clarity, patience, strength), what would it be?"
Saint Ignatius believed that it is important to be aware of "the
grace that you are seeking"—that is, the spiritual gift or virtue
that you need or want at this moment. For example, if your
coworker drove you crazy this morning, you might pray during
the noontime Examen for the grace of patience. If you were hurt
by something a loved one said to you this morning, you might
pray for the grace of patience or peace or temperance—whatever
virtue you need to keep from allowing the hurt feelings to lead
you to think or act inappropriately. If you were tempted toward
some particular sin this morning, you might pray for the grace of
fortitude, of fidelity, or of spiritual discipline.

1. I begin in my usual way.

2. I spend a few moments in gratitude, thanking God for
   one or two of the blessings, big and small, that I've
   received today: the good mood I woke up in, a kind word

---

5. For more on *graces*, see "Important Ignatian Terms," p. 81.

from a friend, my undeserved good health, an easy commute to work, another day with my wonderful spouse.

3. I ask God to show me the greatest challenge I faced today. How did I meet that challenge? Did I respond in *spiritual freedom* or *unfreedom*? What were the consequences of my thoughts, feelings, words, and actions? If I feel moved to do so, I give thanks, I ask forgiveness, I ask for healing.

4. Now, I look to my spirit at this very moment. Right now, how am I feeling about this challenge? I tell God about my feelings and listen for any response from God.

5. I ask the Lord to show me what grace or virtue I may need to meet this challenge tomorrow and in the future (for example: patience, fortitude, courage, generosity, peace of mind and heart). Looking at the past few days, I ask the Lord to show me what ways I am not being open to this grace. I ask the Lord for forgiveness and strength to be open to this grace from this moment forward.

6. I allow myself to daydream about being "filled up" with this grace. What might tomorrow be like if I have this grace with me at all times? I *praydream*—that is, I prayerfully daydream—about the joyful moment when I meet this challenge in a grace-filled way.[6]

7. I ask God to give me the grace I need to be the person he is calling me to be. I repeat the name of this grace over and over again before God. I try to sense God quietly

---

6. For more on "praydream," see "Important Ignatian Terms," p. 81.

filling me with this grace. I praise God for the graces he bestows on me.

8. If I feel moved to do so, I make a resolution to be the kind of person I feel called to be.

9. I end in my usual way.

Examen 4
A Particular Relationship

Rather than reflecting on this past day, today's Examen leads you to ponder the long-term dynamics of one particular relationship in your life.

1. I begin in my usual way.

2. I spend a few moments in gratitude, thanking God for one or two of the blessings, big and small, that I've received today: the good mood I woke up in, a kind word from a friend, my undeserved good health, an easy commute to work, another day with my wonderful spouse.

3. Looking over the recent past, I ask God to show me the person who has been on my mind and in my heart a lot. Odds are, one particular person will rise to the surface of my consciousness pretty quickly. I get a good picture of this person in my mind's eye. I hear the voice, recognize the gestures, and so on.

4. I speculate with God why this person has been so prominent in my attention lately. It might be obvious—for example, we are in the midst of an argument—or it might not be so obvious. I speak with God about this relationship.

5. I ask God to reveal my strongest emotion as I reflect on my relationship with this person. Great love?

Ambivalence? Gratitude? Anger? Attachment? Hurt? Worry? Confusion? I speak with God about how I feel at this very moment. I allow myself to be immersed in this emotion for a moment, and I present this to God. I remain receptive to whatever God might say or do.

6. I ask God to give me a sweeping overview of my relationship with this person. This is not a thorough blow-by-blow analysis. It is a quiet, contemplative "backing up" so that I can see the forest of this relationship rather than getting lost in the trees of it. On the whole, what has this relationship meant to me? Regardless of what is happening now, has this relationship been life-giving or draining? Has it led me closer to God and his way or further from it? Am I more or less faithful, hopeful, and loving because of this relationship? What has been the most difficult part of being in this relationship? What has been the most enjoyable or life-giving part? Finally, is the strong emotion that I'm feeling regarding the present moment (the trees) in sync with the strong emotions I feel as I reflect on the relationship as a whole (the forest)? I speak with God about all of this, listening as much as speaking, should God choose to say something.

7. Still reflecting on the forest, I ask God to show me my own emotions and desires regarding the future of this relationship. What are my great concerns or fears about this relationship? What are my great *desires*[7] for this relationship? What are my hopes and dreams? I speak with God about this. If I desire something in particular, I

---

7. For more on *desires*, see "Important Ignatian Terms," p. 81.

explicitly ask God for this. For example, "Lord, help us to overcome ____ and to focus on ____."

8. Now, I go back to the trees of the present moment. Given my reflection on the forest, has my perspective shifted or have my emotions changed regarding the issues of the day? What specifically am I called to do tomorrow for or with this person? I speak with God about this. If called to do so, I make a particular commitment to think, speak, or act in a certain way. I ask God for help to keep this commitment.

9. I end in my usual way.

Examen 5
Hidden Inner Truths

If you are like me, at any given moment there are little truths about your life that lie beneath the surface of your consciousness—things you have not yet recognized or acknowledged. For me, these hidden truths are usually, but not always, a painful reality that I have trouble accepting. Sometimes there are felicitous happenings in my life that I simply haven't slowed down enough to notice and name. This Examen tries to dig deeply into our thoughts, emotions, behaviors, and motivations to try to uncover a hidden truth or two.

One thing to bear in mind before you begin is that sometimes the really important hidden inner truth is difficult to bring to the level of consciousness and will resist any attempt to do so. Sometimes it's just hard for us to admit an inner truth that is having its way with us. In these cases, your psyche will try a diversion tactic to keep you off the trail; it may reveal a less threatening inner truth to keep you occupied for the duration of the Examen. Therefore, I recommend that you not be satisfied with the first couple of inner truths that surface. Keep digging for a few minutes before you settle on the one you think is most important, which may well be the third or fourth one that comes to mind.

1. I begin in my usual way.

2. I spend a few moments in gratitude, thanking God for one or two of the blessings, big and small, that I've received today: the good mood I woke up in, a kind word from a friend, my undeserved good health, an easy commute to work, another day with my wonderful spouse.

3. I ask God to reveal to me any hidden truths about any of the important relationships in my life. For example, "I didn't realize it, but . . ."

   - I'm angry with _____.
   - I'm attracted to _____.
   - I'm getting along better with _____.
   - I'm not so angry with _____. I seem to have forgiven her and not noticed!
   - I'm afraid of _____'s outbursts.
   - I'm trying to impress _____.

4. If a large and striking revelation occurs to me, one that makes me go, "Wow, I hadn't noticed that before" or "Well, I guess it's time to admit the truth of that," then I remain on that one hidden truth for the rest of the Examen. If nothing big shows up when I muse over my relationships, then I move on to my subconscious thoughts, feelings, and attitudes about recent events in my life, about any attachments I'm clinging to, and about my own relationship with myself. For example, "I didn't realize it, but . . ."

- I'm sad about _____ moving away.
- I'm not as anxious about that daunting task at the office.
- I'm worried about our finances.
- I'm spending more and more time on useless web browsing.
- I'm clinging too tightly to owning _____, when perhaps God or my life circumstances call me to let it go.
- I'm getting older and am not admitting it to myself.
- I'm not as bad at _____ as I think I am.
- Despite my pessimism, things are turning out OK.

5. When I have settled on the most important inner truth, I let go of all of the others and simply have a conversation with God about this one reality in my life. I summarize it in one simple statement such as one of the examples above, and I make that statement over and over again to God, letting its reality and existence sink in and not hide again.

6. I note what emotions I am feeling as I make this statement to God. What is the strongest emotion that I feel as I name this truth to God? I now add this to my statement. For example, "Lord, I feel _____ as I admit that _____." I let myself steep in that emotion for a while and I keep presenting to God both the truth and its accompanying emotion.

7. I get really quiet now and try to detect if God is trying to say or do something about this reality. How does God feel about this truth? How does God feel about how *I*

feel? If I feel called to do so, I listen for God's message to me or I await his touch on my heart. I ask God, "What is it you would have me do about this? How should this truth affect who I am?" I listen for what might be an answer from God.

8. If I feel called to do so, I make a commitment to God about this. I ask God for help to be faithful to my commitment.

9. I end in my usual way.

Present or Absent?

God calls us to be fully present to the moment at hand, but so often we are lost in another world, lost in the past, lost in the future, lost in our broodings, lost even in our joys. Or perhaps we just get lost in the latest silly game on our smart phones while someone or some task needs our full attention. Today's Examen invites you to explore the ways in which you were present and in which you were absent to the moments of your day.

1. I begin in my usual way.

2. I spend a few moments in gratitude, thanking God for one or two of the blessings, big and small, that I've received today.

3. Looking through my day, I ask the Lord to show me the moments when I was not fully present—when I became distracted and lost in my own thoughts or perhaps was working or playing with something else while the moment called for my full attention. I ask God to show me the ill effects of my absence and to show me how much better things could have gone had I been fully present. I speak with God about those moments. I ask God for advice, healing, forgiveness.

4. As I look through the day, I also recognize the grace-filled moments when I was fully present to the present. Perhaps

it was a moment when someone really needed a listening ear or a helping hand, and I had the grace to step in. Perhaps it was a difficult or complicated task, and I had the grace to focus really well on the situation. Or maybe it simply was a moment when I was fully cognizant of the goodness that dwelled in the room: inside me, inside the others around me, in the very air that we breathed. I pause and give thanks to God for those grace-filled moments.

5. I now look to tomorrow. What moment tomorrow could really use my full attention? In which moment may I be tempted to get lost in thought or lost in some diversion? I speak with God about the concrete moments that might challenge my full presence tomorrow.

6. I end in my usual way.

Examen 7

A Shift in My Spirit

You can use this particular Examen to reflect on the big picture or on the small picture. You can reflect on anything from a subtle shift in your day to a big change in your disposition over the past few years. You may want to use this Examen at moments of transition, such as the end of a semester or on New Year's Day.

1. I begin in my usual way.

2. I spend a few moments in gratitude, thanking God for one or two of the blessings, big and small, that I've received today.

3. Looking over the past few weeks, months, or even years, I ask God for the *grace* to see any shift that may have occurred in my spirit. For example, have I grown despondent lately? Have I snapped at people more frequently? Am I quieter than I used to be? Am I more at peace? Do I laugh more? Do I sleep better or worse than I used to? Have I grown confident? lazy? anxious? needy? prayerful? loving? forgiving? despairing? pessimistic? hopeful? preoccupied? fearful? relaxed? bitter? accepting? In what way have I changed?

4. I may identify several shifts in my spirit, but I ask God to reveal to me the most influential one. I zoom in on that one. Has this been a good shift? a bad shift? or a mixed

bag? I ask God to show me how this shift has played a role in my life. I ask God to show me his perspective on it. I ask God to show me how he has been present in this shift. I also ponder: In what ways has this shift *not* been from God?

5. I ask for forgiveness for and healing from any part of this that is not from God.

6. If this shift has had a good impact on my life, then I spend some long moments in thanksgiving: "Thank you for the growth, Lord." "Thank you for healing this wound." "Thank you for giving me the grace to move on." "Thank you for letting me feel more confident in myself."

7. I ask God to show me what I am called to do about this shift. Should I "feed the shift," working toward growing further in this direction? Should I "shift the shift," working toward changing course—adjusting my attitude, changing my behavior, and so on? Is there anyone, such as my spouse or my spiritual director, whom I should speak to about this shift? What am I called to do? *Who* am I called to be?

8. If I feel called to do so, I make a promise to God to do what I'm called to do, to be who I'm called to be in this area of my life.

9. I end in my usual way.

Examen 8

Am I Ready to Die Today?

1. I begin in my usual way.[8]

2. I spend a few moments in gratitude, thanking God for one or two of the blessings, big and small, that I've received today.

3. I ask God to help me explore the question: *Am I ready to die today?* Knowing that God is all-loving and desires me to be with him for eternity, am I ready to join him in heaven?

4. If I knew that I would die within the next twenty-four hours, what would I want to do with my last day in order to be ready? What would it take for me to do or say the things that would prepare me for death? What *graces* would I want or need from God?

5. Now I tease out these ideas a bit more. I *praydream* (prayerfully daydream) what it would be like to say and do those very things that keep me from being ready to die. I watch a little movie in my mind in which I live out the concrete things that I've discerned to do. How might it go? What would be the first steps I would take toward being ready to die? I ask God for the graces required to accomplish this.

---

8. The original idea for this Examen comes from Michael Schonhoff.

6. If I feel called to do so, I make a promise to God to say or do something specific and concrete within the next twenty-four hours that will prepare me for eternal life.

7. I end in my usual way.

An Interior Wound

If you and I are honest, at any given moment we can probably identify a wound or two within us. A wound is some emotional hurt in my heart, psyche, or soul caused by something painful that has happened. Maybe you were insulted by someone. You felt rejected. You were fired from your job. You were unappreciated. This Examen leads us to pray about these wounds.

Quickly read through the whole thing before beginning this Examen. Note that it is a particularly challenging one. If you're not in the right space for it (for example, you're having a bad day, or you're doing this Examen in a very public place, or you've been down lately and you fear this might make it worse), then you might want to pass over this one until a day comes when you are ready for it.

1. I begin in my usual way.

2. I spend a few moments in gratitude, thanking God for one or two of the blessings, big and small, that I've received today.

3. I ask God to show me a wound in my heart at this moment. This wound causes me to feel hurt, frightened, angry, resentful, or remorseful. I allow God to take me to that difficult place in my soul. Perhaps I find myself painfully—but also prayerfully—remembering the

moments that have created this wound. I courageously sit in the midst of this difficult moment. Perhaps I ask Jesus to hold my hand as I prayerfully relive the worst parts.

4. I ask God to show me the strongest emotion I have at this very moment as I rehash this painful experience. I speak aloud to God about how I am feeling. I say, "God, I am furious (or sad, or grief-stricken, or confused)." I sit with God and with these feelings for a moment.

5. I ask God to show me how this wound might become worse—growing in size or becoming infected. If I were to allow this wound to lead me away from faith, hope, and love, what might that look like? Concretely, in what ways might this wound tempt me to behave poorly? I ask God to help me prevent this from happening. If I need a particular *grace* to help me guard against this poor behavior, I ask for that grace from God right now.

6. I sit in the silence for just a moment, giving God a chance to do whatever God wants with me right now. Perhaps, in this quiet moment, God will just place his warm fatherly hand on my head. Perhaps God will say something to me. Perhaps we'll just sit together in the silence. It's OK if God seems to be saying and doing nothing at all. I trust that he will heal this wound in his own time and his own way.

7. I prayerfully daydream for just a moment, imagining a day when I am no longer feeling wounded about this. What would that be like? What might be my attitudes, perspectives, thoughts, feelings, words, and actions if I

were truly a recovered soul? What *grace* would I need to begin to heal? I ask God for that grace right now.

8. I ask God to show me how he might make good come out of this hurtful thing. How can this wound make me stronger? More loving? More humble? More spiritually mature? How can I become a more effective disciple of God's love through this wound? I ask God to make good use of this wound—to use this experience of mine for his greater glory.

9. If I feel called to do so, I make some concrete resolution to be a person of faith, hope, and love in the midst of this painful reality in my life. I trust that God will be there with me through it all.

10. I end in my usual way.

Examen 10
Habits

Aristotle once said, "We are what we repeatedly do. Excellence, then, is not an act but a habit." Aristotle believed that the key to living a good life is to develop good habits. Humans are very much creatures of habit. God made us this way so that we don't have to rely solely on good judgment and decision making in each situation that arises. Instead, we can train our minds, bodies, and souls to habitually, naturally do the right thing. Unfortunately, we can just as easily fall into unhealthy habits! Today's Examen encourages a reflection on habits.

1. I begin in my usual way.

2. I spend a few moments in gratitude, thanking God for one or two of the blessings, big and small, that I've received today: the good mood I woke up in, a kind word from a friend, my undeserved good health, an easy commute to work, another day with my wonderful spouse.

3. Looking over my day, I ask God to show me a few of my habits. I try to see my one thought or action today that is actually typical of the way I think or act. For example, I may find myself saying to Christ, "Lord, looking over my day, I see that I am in the habit of . . ."

- criticizing and nitpicking my coworkers
- staying focused on my work, once I've had a strong cup of coffee
- putting myself down for the smallest things
- wasting time on the Internet
- greeting people warmly when they walk in the door

4. It's usually easier to see my unhealthy habits than to see the healthy ones. When I do find an unhealthy habit, I speak with God about it. Perhaps I'll ask God for forgiveness, or for healing, and for ideas about how to break the habit.

5. But I don't want to settle for simply looking at my bad habits. I won't rest until I find a couple of good habits in my day today. When I do find them, I will give thanks and praise. I speak to God about why I'm so grateful for this good habit.

6. I now look to tomorrow. What bad habit do I want to break? What good habit do I want to cultivate? What *graces* will I ask God for in order to help me break these particular bad habits and grow these particular good habits? I speak with God about this.

7. I end in my usual way.

Examen 11
Saving F. A.C.E.

This Examen is based on the ideas of David Richo, who observes that many of our problems stem from saving F. A.C.E.—that is, being dictated by our Fears, Attachments, need for Control, and illusions of Entitlement.

Quickly read through the whole thing before beginning this Examen. Note that it is a particularly challenging one. If you're not in the right space for it—you're having a bad day, you're doing this Examen in a very public place, you've been down lately and you fear this might make it worse—then you might want to pass over this one until a day comes when you are ready for it.

1. I begin in my usual way.

2. I spend a few moments in gratitude, thanking God for one or two of the blessings, big and small, that I've received today.

3. I spend a little extra time asking God for a double-dose of *grace* to pray this particularly difficult Examen. It is difficult because it demands that I look at some of the darker parts of my personality. I will ask God to show me ways in which I have tried to save F. A.C.E. recently. I can easily fall into one of two traps: either denying that I have a problem or unlovingly condemning myself. I need the

extra grace to allow God to lead in a firm but unconditionally loving way.

4. Looking over my day, I ask God to show me what **Fears** were predominant in my heart. I try to dig deeply and see what I am *really* afraid of (it may not be what I expect because our true fears are often hidden beneath our level of consciousness). As soon as I name that fear, I simply take note of it and move to the next step.

5. Looking over my day, I ask God to show me any **Attachments** to which I've been clinging lately. I might be overly attached to a person (infatuated), to an idea (stubborn), or to a behavior (bad habit). I pay particular attention to my *emotional* attachment to people, ideas, or behaviors. Once I've identified a particular attachment, I take note of it and move on to the next step.

6. Looking over my day, I ask God to show me any situation in which I'm trying too hard to exert **Control**. I may be trying to control people, organizations, or outcomes. It's difficult to admit that I'm controlling, so I ask God for the courage to do so. When I find my particular obsession with control, I simply acknowledge it and move to the next step.

7. Looking over my day, I ask God to show me if I have any silly notions of **Entitlement**. For example: "I worked hard today, I deserve this doughnut / this drink / this cigarette." Or "I'm an important person; I'm entitled to skip my share of the chores, the menial tasks, the grunt work." Or "I'm the victim here. I have a right to blow up, to

pout, to be passive, to feel sorry for myself." If I find a false Entitlement, I name it before God and move on.

8. Now, I place before God the four discoveries I've made: one Fear, one Attachment, one need to Control, and one Entitlement. I ask God to show me which of the four is most strongly affecting my life right now. I zoom in on that one issue and leave the other three behind. I ask God for insight. I ask for forgiveness for the times when I've let it get the best of me.

9. I ask God to show me what *tomorrow* may look like if I acted out of freedom from this issue. In specific terms, how would my day be different if I didn't allow this issue to rule me? How would my emotions, thoughts, words, and actions be different?

10. I give this issue to God. I say, "Lord, today I wish to turn over my _____ to you. I ask you to take over and become the Lord of my life, rather than letting this issue lord over me." I ask God to help me live my life in the freedom of God's mercy.

11. I end in my usual way.

Examen 12

Who Wore God's Face Today?

1. I begin in my usual way.

2. I spend a few moments in gratitude, thanking God for one or two of the blessings, big and small, that I've received today.

3. I look back on my day and ask God, "Who wore your face for me today? At what moment did you come to me through the words or actions of another person?" I relish that moment. I give thanks and praise for the gift of that person in my life.

4. I look again at my day and ask God, "In what person did I fail to find your presence? What person did I judge to be without goodness?" I relive that difficult moment in my mind, speaking with God about why that moment was so difficult for me. I say to God whatever wells up in my heart. I ask for wisdom. I beg forgiveness. I ask for healing. I ask how God was hidden in this person and how I might call forth that Presence the next time that I encounter that person.

5. I look again at my day and ask God, "Was there some person I encountered today who needed *me* to be your hands? your feet? your voice? your presence? Did I succeed in manifesting your presence for this person?" I try

to identify one person for whom I failed to be God's presence. I ask for wisdom, forgiveness, healing. I then try to come up with one person for whom I did succeed at being the presence of God. I relish this moment, giving thanks for it.

6. I ask God to show me a person who might really need me to be God's presence the next time I encounter her or him. I *praydream* that moment—that is, I play out in my *prayerful imagination*[9] how it might go if I truly am able to manifest God's presence for this person tomorrow or the next day. I try to identify one *grace* I might need to make this happen. I ask God for this grace right now.

7. If I feel called to do so, I promise God to do a particular thing based on what I've prayed about during this Examen.

8. I end in my usual way.

---

9. For more on *prayerful imagination*, see "Important Ignatian Terms," p. 81.

Examen 13
Thoughts, Words, Deeds

1. I begin in my usual way.

2. I spend a few moments in gratitude, thanking God for one or two of the blessings, big and small, that I've received today.

3. I ask God to reveal to me my **thoughts** of this day. What were my strongest thoughts? What strong opinions did I hold? What attitudes did I carry with me? What presumptions did I make? How did I perceive myself, my situation, the people, places, and events of my day? What conclusions did I make?

4. When I come upon a strong and influential thought that I had today, I sit with it for a moment. What was the source of this thought? Did it come from a place of *spiritual freedom* or from a place of unfreedom? Did it lead me to greater or lesser spiritual freedom? Did it lead me to greater faith, hope, and love or lesser faith, hope, and love?

5. I give thanks for the thoughts that came from the true Spirit, and I ask forgiveness if I allowed unfreedoms within me to influence my thoughts.

6. I repeat steps 3–5, this time reviewing my **words**. I ask God to show me the strongest or most important words

that I spoke today. I ponder the source of my words. I give thanks or ask forgiveness whenever appropriate.

7. I repeat steps 3–5, this time reviewing my **deeds**. What did I do that was loving and kind? What did I do that was unloving and unhelpful? What motivated my deeds? I give thanks or ask forgiveness where needed.

8. I now look to tomorrow. What *thoughts* and attitudes do I *desire* to hold tomorrow? About myself? About the people around me? About the situations I encounter? What do I desire to *say* tomorrow to the specific people I'll probably encounter? What do I desire to *do* tomorrow? What deeds of love am I called to perform? I listen for God's voice.

9. I make some concrete resolution based on what arose in this prayer time.

10. I end in my usual way.

Examen 14

My Emotions

1. I begin in my usual way.

2. I spend a few moments in gratitude, thanking God for one or two of the blessings, big and small, that I've received today.

3. Instead of reviewing my day hour by hour, I ask God to review my day emotion by emotion. God and I watch and observe as my emotional state progresses through the day. How did I feel when I woke up this morning? As I was showering, eating breakfast, dressing for the day? How did I feel when I began the tasks of the day? As the morning progressed? And so on. I quickly pass over the fleeting emotions but dwell on the more pervasive ones or those I hadn't noticed before. I also speak with God as I notice shifts in my emotions throughout the day.

4. I speak with God about the strongest emotions of the day. Were they of the good spirit—that is, the part of me that is moving closer to God and deeper in faith, hope, and love? Were they of the false spirit—the spirit in me that is stuck in earthly thoughts, desires, cravings, or obsessions?

5. I choose the strongest emotion of the day, and I speak to God about the way I responded to that emotion as the

day progressed. I review the impact this emotion had on me. Did I even acknowledge the emotion as I experienced it, or was I unaware of it? Did I consciously choose how to act on this emotion, or did I allow the emotion to choose how I would think, speak, and act throughout the day? I speak with God about this, thanking God when my response to the emotion was in sync with my Christian calling, and asking for forgiveness and healing when my response was not.

6. Knowing that my emotions are only partially in my control, I reflect on what emotions I want to have tomorrow. If I could choose only one, what would it be: joy? peace? loving-kindness? courage? gratitude? I pick one of these and imagine myself living out tomorrow with this emotion as my companion. I ask God to grant me the *grace* to be open to this emotion tomorrow and to put it to good use if and when it does come.

7. I end in my usual way.

Examen 15

Gratitude

St. Ignatius believed that gratitude was among the highest of virtues. In fact, he believed that ingratitude was the root of all sin. And it stands to reason: sin is basically a misuse of the gifts God has given us. If we are truly grateful for the gift, then we certainly won't consciously misuse it.

This particular Examen has you spend the entire time naming the blessings in your life and thanking God for each one of them. Any time is a good time to praise and thank God, but I especially recommend this Examen when you are feeling down, having a bad day, or being unusually self-critical.

1. I begin in my usual way.

2. I ask God to reveal, in a special way today, all the blessings of my life—the really big ones and the small ones, too.

3. I ask myself, "What am I most grateful for today? What is it that fills me with joy and gratitude?" Usually, one person, place, event, or thing will pop up immediately. I name this gift before God: "Lord, I am so grateful for your gift to me of ___." I simply repeat this over and over for a moment, letting the gratitude sink deep.

4. I relish this one gift for a while. If I am most grateful for my sister, for example, I place her lovely face before my

mind's eye. I see her smile; I watch one of her gestures or facial expressions that always tickles me or warms my heart. And I just sit there, filled with love. All the while, I say, "Thank you, Lord." It doesn't have to be a person. On any given day, I may be grateful for a thing or an organization. I may be grateful for my warm and cozy house and the comfort that it brings when I return home every day. I may be thankful for my church community or for the company I work for. Perhaps I am most grateful for something that happened recently. For example, I may find myself filled with gratitude because someone who is normally unkind to me had a good disposition toward me. Maybe I'm grateful for receiving a raise, a good peer review, or a high grade on a test. Whatever it is, I relish this gift by placing it before me in *prayerful imagination*. I allow the good feelings to well up and overflow within me, all the while saying, "Thank you, Lord" in my heart.

5. I now more lightly watch a long and boisterous parade of gifts go by in my imagination and thank God for each one. One by one, in chaotic and random order, the big and small gifts of my life float before my mind's eye: my health—"Thank you, Lord"; my relatives (even the difficult ones!)—"Thank you, Lord"; my neighbor—"Thank you, Lord"; my talent for making people laugh—"Thank you, Lord"; the exotic meal I successfully cooked last night—"Thank you, Lord." On and on and on—a Thanksgiving parade to rival Macy's!

6. I end in my usual way.

Examen 16

Clinging? Avoiding? or Just Right?

1. I begin in my usual way.

2. I spend a few moments in gratitude, thanking God for one or two of the blessings, big and small, that I've received today.

3. Sitting in God's presence, I look over my past day, searching for any person, place, thing, or activity to which I am **clinging** too tightly. To whom or what am I too attached? addicted to? too dependent on? I don't allow myself to be satisfied with the first example I find. I dig deeply and see if I can find two or three answers to this question. When I land on the most important one, I spend time speaking with God about this. I ask God for advice, forgiveness, or healing.

4. With God, I return to my sweep over the day, this time searching for any person, place, thing, or activity I am **avoiding**. From whom or what am I running? actively ignoring? resisting? pushing out of my life? Again, I work diligently at this search until I have found not one but two or three answers. I then speak with God about the most important one. Again, I ask God for advice, forgiveness, and healing. I listen quietly, waiting for God to respond.

5. With God, I return to my day a third time, this time searching for any person, place, thing, or activity to which my relationship is **just right**. Which gift of God do I seem to be using just as God would want me to? For example, "My marriage is suddenly going just right these days! Thank you!" Or "I like my job, but today I didn't let it keep me from coaching my kid's soccer game. Thanks, Lord." In other words, what went right today, and what person, place, thing, or activity do I have to thank for it? I give praise to the Creator of all good gifts.

6. Finally, I sweep back over this prayer time. What moment was the most enlightening or moving? I return to that moment and speak with God a second time about it. I dwell on this important point for a while. I now look to tomorrow. Given what I've experienced in this Examen, do I feel called to make any changes in my thoughts, words, or actions? If so, I commit to doing so. I ask God for help to do what I've decided to do.

7. I end in my usual way.

Praise, Reverence, Service

We are created to praise, reverence, and serve God our Lord, and by this means to save our souls. And the other things on the face of the earth are created for us and that they may help us in prosecuting the end for which we are created. From this it follows that we are to use them as much as they help us on to our end, and ought to rid ourselves of them so far as they hinder us as to it.

—St. Ignatius of Loyola, The First Principle and Foundation

1. I begin in my usual way.

2. I now spend a while in **praise**. I start by slowly, quietly saying to God, "I praise you, Lord . . . I praise you, Lord . . . I praise you, Lord."

3. I then move to praising God for the gifts he's given me this very day: "I praise you for your gift of my family . . . I praise you for the gift of my job . . . I praise you for my *desire* to serve you."

4. I then move to praising God for his attributes, which have shown up in my day: "I praise you for your mercy—for forgiving me today when I _____. I praise you for your kindness to me today, when I was depressed and you were present to me in the way I needed and right when I needed it. I praise you for your providence, when

everything turned out OK during our little crisis this morning."

5. I now spend a while in **reverence**. I acknowledge that God is bigger than everything, even the things that appear so big to me today. For example, "You, God, are bigger than my career. You, God, are bigger than my worry over _____ today. You, God, are bigger than my failure of _____ today or my success over _____ today. You, God, are bigger than my love for _____ today. You, God, are bigger than my craving for _____ today."

6. I now spend a while in commitment to **Christian service**. I look to the specific people, places, tasks, and happenings of tomorrow, and I pray: "Lord, help me serve you by loving _____ well. Help me serve you by working diligently on _____. Help me serve you through my talent of _____. Help me serve you through my fidelity to _____. Help me serve you by treating _____ with _____."

7. I end in my usual way.

God, Others, Self

1. I begin in my usual way.

2. I spend a few moments in gratitude, thanking God for one or two of the blessings, big and small, that I've received today.

3. I reflect on my **relationship with God**. I talk to God about it. How is our relationship going? Have we been getting along well? Do I feel close to or distant from God right now? Have I spent quality time with God or have I been neglectful? Do I get a sense that God is very close to me when I call on him? Am I bored with God? When I look upon the "face" of God, do I feel joy? gratitude? shame? fear? I speak with God about our relationship. I ask God to reveal to me his perspective on our relationship.

4. I talk to God about my **relationship with others** at this moment. How has my disposition been lately when I am around others? grumpy? friendly? passive? affirming? Is there a particular relationship that has been unusually good or unusually sour? I speak with God about this. I ask God to show me his perspective on it.

5. I talk to God about how my **relationship with myself** has been going lately. Do I like myself nowadays? Am I

proud of myself? Mad at myself? Tender with myself? Harsh with myself? What factors in my life have led to these attitudes and behaviors toward myself? I speak with God about this. I ask God for his perspective on it.

6. I now look over these past three reflections: relationship with God, relationship with others, relationship with self. Which of the three moments felt most powerful to me as I reflected on it? In which of these moments did I have the strongest emotional response as I reflected upon the relationship? I revisit that one relationship, asking God for forgiveness, giving God thanks, asking God to give me some insight to help me move forward in this relationship or to reveal to me some truth about this relationship I have not noticed or acknowledged before now.

7. I ask God, "What would you like me to do about this relationship as I move forward? What gradual shifts might I initiate? What parts of the relationship might I nurture? Which parts might I let go of or even put a stop to?"

8. I ask God, "What specifically can I do tomorrow regarding this relationship?"

9. If appropriate, I make a commitment to God about how I may proceed in the future of this relationship. I ask God for the help to keep this commitment.

10. I end in my usual way.

Examen 19

What Was Draining?
What Was Life-Giving?

1. I begin in my usual way.[10]

2. I spend a few moments in gratitude, thanking God for one or two of the blessings, big and small, that I've received today.

3. Looking back over the day, I ask God to reveal to me which moment was the most draining. In my *imagination*, God and I return to that draining moment and I relive it—this time with God right beside me. I let myself become steeped in the moment, particularly in the most difficult thing about that moment. I let myself feel the strong emotions—lethargy, despair, and whatever other feelings are present in me. I present this draining moment to God, and I especially speak to God about what was going on in my heart and soul in that moment. If I handled it OK, then I thank God for that. If I handled it badly, I ask for pardon and peace.

4. I ask God to speak to me about this moment. I remain receptive to anything God says or does.

5. Looking over my day a second time, I ask God to reveal the most life-giving moment of the day. I again return

---

10. The original idea for this Examen comes from Dianne Hanley.

with God to that moment, reliving both the exterior events and my interior dispositions. Steeped in joy, gratitude, and relief, I give it all to God. I talk with God about it, making sure to express my thoughts and feelings and to let God speak freely to me.

6. I now look to tomorrow. What may be a draining moment of tomorrow? (Most of the time, we all have a pretty good guess about this.) I speak with God about this. I tell God how I feel about this possibility; I ask God to show me how I can spiritually prepare for this potentially draining moment. I ask God to keep me from contributing negatively to the situation by presuming the worst. I allow for the possibility that everything will go fine. I pray for the virtue of hope.

7. I look to tomorrow a second and final time. What may be the most life-giving moment? I allow myself to get excited about this moment. I let myself fill up with good and wholesome *desires* about it. I tell God all about it. I let whatever happens happen. I ask God to help me spiritually prepare for the possibility that it won't be as life-giving as I hope. I ask God for the ability to say, "That would be OK, too."

8. I end in my usual way.

Examen 20

A Discernment

1. I begin in my usual way.

2. I spend a few moments in gratitude, thanking God for one or two of the blessings, big and small, that I've received today.

3. I ask God to reveal some decision I need to make. It could be a small decision I'll be making shortly—for example, how to handle a tricky situation; whether to say yes or no to an invitation; or what to say to someone asking my advice. Or it could be a big decision that is more long-term: a career choice; initiating a significant change in a relationship; making an important commitment. I ask God to lay out the options before me.

4. I ask God to show me how the factors related to this decision have affected my life in the recent past. I ask God to show me if leaning toward one or another direction has led to greater faith, hope, and love in my life. Has one direction led me closer to God? Has one direction seemed to lead me to a peace that could come only from God?

5. I ask God to reveal how this decision might affect the people involved. Will it help them or hurt them? If it will

hurt them, is there some higher good that will come from it that would make it worth the hurt?

6. I ask God to show me my own emotions regarding this decision, particularly any emotions I've not yet acknowledged. For each strong emotion, I ask God to reveal the source of the emotion. Is it coming from a good spirit or a bad spirit within me? In other words, is this emotion coming from the part of me that is in sync with God or from the part of me that is running from or opposing God?

7. I surrender this whole matter to God, saying, "Thy will be done, O Lord." I ask God to give me a sense of peace about the whole thing, right now. I ask him to take me to the place in my heart that is beyond my emotions so that I may see the situation from a more objective point of view.

8. If I feel called to make a decision right now, I place that decision before God and ask him to make good of it, even if it is a mistake. If I am called to continue discerning for a while longer, I ask God for the patience to sit and wait for his call. If it is a big decision, I take note of the direction in which God seems to be leading me at this moment and I note whether or not this seems to be the way God has been nudging me for a while now.

9. I close this Examen in my usual way, or perhaps by quietly whispering, over and over again: "Thy will be done, Lord . . . Thy will be done, Lord . . . Thy will be done, Lord."

As I Do to the Least . . .

*Just as you did it to one of the least of these who are members of
my family, you did it to me.*
—Matthew 25:40

1. I begin in my usual way.

2. I spend a few moments in gratitude, thanking God for
   one or two of the blessings, big and small, that I've
   received today.

3. I ask God, "Of the people I encountered today, who was
   the most outcast? The weakest and most fragile? The
   most difficult for me to be around?" In my imagination, I
   replay the moment when I encountered that person.

4. I speak to God about my observations. I tell God my
   thoughts, words, and actions toward that person. I ask
   God for forgiveness for any thoughts, words, or actions
   that were unkind or uncharitable. I thank God for the
   moments when I seemed to have the right disposition.

5. I ask God, "What do you see when you see this person?
   What do you have to say to me about this person?"

6. I ask God, "What am I called to do for this person? Who
   am I called to *be* for this person?"

7. I get more concrete and specific: "God, what, if anything,
   am I called to do or be for this person *tomorrow*?" I ask
   God to give me the ability to do these things.

8. If I feel called to do so, I make some sort of resolution.

9. I end in my usual way.

Examen 22

Repulsions, Inspirations, Desires

1. I begin in my usual way.

2. I spend a few moments in gratitude, thanking God for one or two of the blessings, big and small, that I've received today.

3. Looking back on my day, I ask God to show me the moments in which I was **repulsed** by someone or something. To be repulsed means to feel uncontrollably driven to reject or flee from that person or thing. When did that happen today? What person did I encounter that led me to feel disgust? fear? anger? loathing? Was there some incident, task, place, discussion, or thing that drove me to want to run the other way or to react violently? I speak to God about this. I pray to God for forgiveness, advice, and healing.

4. I look over my day a second time, asking God to reveal the moments I felt **inspired** to do something good or to be someone noble. Did I encounter someone today who inspired me? Did something happen today that filled me with good and holy passion and warmth? Did I see, hear, or experience something that made me feel that way? I speak to God about this. I give thanks and praise for this moment.

5. I look at my day one last time, asking God to bring to mind the moments in which I felt filled with **great desires**. By great desires I mean desires to do good and holy things, and to be a good and holy person. Great desires are those God plants in my heart; they are ultimately desires for faith, hope, and love. Was there a moment today when I felt such desires, even if I wasn't fully conscious of it at the time? Was there a moment today when I thought about the future with wholesome and loving dreams? Was there a moment when I day-dreamed a future for myself filled with God's presence and filled with faith, hope, and love? I speak to God about this. I thank and praise God for this moment. I ask God if this moment truly came from him, and I pause in silence to listen for a response. I am open and receptive to God's response to me, whatever it is.

6. I now review my prayer time and these three reflections of repulsions, inspirations, and desires. Of the three reflections, which one has most enlightened or moved me? I return to that moment and linger there awhile. What is the primary emotion I feel as I reflect on this? I tell God about how I'm feeling right at this moment, and I listen for God's response. I talk with God about it, or perhaps we just sit there in the blessedness of this sacred moment.

7. Given my reflection on today, I now look to tomorrow. "Is there anything concrete that you are calling me to do tomorrow, Lord?" "Given my repulsions, inspirations, and desires today, *who* am I called to be tomorrow?"

8. If I feel led to do so, I make some commitment to God about tomorrow. I ask God for the help to fulfill my commitment.

9. I end in my usual way.

Examen 23
Aces and Deuces

This Examen will help you reflect on the "hand of cards" that you have been dealt; in other words, your unique set of gifts and weaknesses.

1. I begin in my usual way.

2. I spend a few moments in gratitude, thanking God for one or two of the blessings, big and small, that I've received today.

3. I reflect on this day in a unique way: I imagine my own thoughts, words, and actions this day to be "my hand of cards" in a poker game. In poker, the aces are the highest ranking cards and the deuces (the twos) are the lowest. Looking at my "hand" of good personal qualities and not-so-good personal qualities that showed up in me today, I ask God, "What are my aces, Lord?" my smarts? my patience? my sense of humor? my passion? my flexibility? my temperance? my listening skills? I ask God to point out two or three of my aces and how they served me and others well as I played my hand today. I speak with God about this. I thank God for the gifts and talents I've been given.

4. I look again at my day, asking God, "What are my deuces, Lord?" being overly serious? impatient? overly

sensitive? restless? anxious? afraid of my own emotions? stubborn? passive? lazy? self-centered? low self-esteem? obsessed with success or with my reputation? I ask God to point out two or three of my deuces and how they hampered me today. I speak with God about this. I ask for help with these difficult cards of mine.

5. I now look to tomorrow. God and I imagine how tomorrow might progress. I think about the people I will see, the tasks I'll be working on, and so on. I ask God to show me how I might play my cards. How might I use my aces for the good of all, and how might I minimize the impact of my deuces? I try to be as concrete as possible. For example, "Because I am patient and my spouse is not, maybe I can handle _____ and let him take care of _____." Or "Because I have low self-esteem, I need to be careful not to play that card (i.e., let it get the best of me) in that crucial presentation that I'm giving tomorrow."

6. If I feel called to make any sort of commitment to God about the specifics of tomorrow, I do so. I ask God for help with this commitment.

7. I end in my usual way.

Examen 24

Surprise!

1. I begin in my usual way.
2. I spend a few moments in gratitude, thanking God for one or two of the blessings, big and small, that I've received today.
3. I ask God to show me a negative surprise from this past day. It may be something really big, such as losing my job or going to the emergency room. It may be something really small, such as feeling under the weather or feeling snubbed by a friend.
4. In my imagination, I replay the moments of my day that were affected by that negative surprise, paying particular attention to both my interior response (attitude/disposition) and my exterior response (words/actions). I ask God for forgiveness for any response that was not from his inspiration. I thank God for any response that was from him.
5. I ask God to show me the biggest positive surprise of my day. It may be something really big, such as passing an important test, or something really small, such as "waking up on the right side of the bed" or getting an unexpected compliment from a coworker.

6. In my *prayerful imagination*, I replay the moment or moments of my day that were affected by that positive surprise, paying particular attention to both my interior response (attitude/disposition) and my exterior response (words/actions). I ask God for forgiveness for any response that was not from God's inspiration (ingratitude, for example), and I thank God for any that was.

7. Now, I look to tomorrow. I ask God to show me a concrete way I could surprise someone tomorrow. It could be something big, such as getting a person a gift or finally apologizing for something I've done wrong but never admitted to. Or it could be something really small, such as not being so grumpy with the coworker who gets under my skin. It could be for a person I love, such as my spouse, or it could be for someone who drives me crazy, like my boss.

8. I ask God to help me *desire* to create this surprising moment. I try to stir up excitement in my heart about it. I imagine the good that will come from it.

9. If I feel called to do so, I resolve to do it and not back out.

10. I end in my usual way.

Examen 25

Thank You for . . . Forgive Me for . . . Help Me with . . .

1. I begin in my usual way.[11]

2. I address God spontaneously regarding the things, people, and moments for which I am most grateful. I say, "Thank you, God, for . . ." and I just let my mind drift from one gift of my life to the next, without consciously steering my thoughts one way or another. I take note of what I find my heart and soul are saying to God at this moment.

3. Next, I talk to God about the things, people, and moments about which I feel bad. I say, "Forgive me, God, for . . ." and I just let myself go. I listen carefully to what I find my heart and soul are saying to God at this moment.

4. Finally, I address God regarding the future things, future people, and future moments for which I will need God's help. Thinking about the coming day, I pray, "God, help me with . . ." and I just let myself go. I attend to what my heart and soul are saying to God at this moment.

5. I end in my usual way.

---

11. The original idea for this Examen comes from Matthew Linn, SJ.

My Greatest Fear

I'm convinced that fear plays a far greater role in our lives than we realize or want to admit. Every year when I go on retreat to pray and rest, I ask myself, "What is my greatest fear at this moment in my life?" It always brings about fruitful dialogue with God.

Today's Examen invites us to go to that dark spot in our hearts and psyches and stare right into the face of our fears. It takes some work and some courage to get to the very bottom of our fears. Often, I discover that the root of my fear is not at all what I would have expected. This spiritual work can be deeply consoling in the end, but it is not for the faint of heart; so I recommend you do this Examen only if you're up for it. Otherwise, save it for another time.

1. I begin in my usual way.

2. I spend a few moments in gratitude, thanking God for one or two of the blessings, big and small, that I've received today.

3. I look over my day and ask God, "Where did fear play a role in my thoughts, words, actions, or inactions?" I will not be satisfied until I come up with an answer to that question. (It may take a while.) After I've located one fear, I look again and see if God is trying to show me one or two other moments when fear played a role. (Often,

the first answer that comes is not the most important one.)

4. Once I have identified the most important fear, I zoom in on it. What am I afraid of? I say out loud to God: "Lord, I am afraid of ___." What exactly is so scary about this? What is the most frightening thing about it? (What I'm trying to do here is get to the deeper fears beneath the superficial ones. For example, "I'm afraid of upsetting the boss" might lead to "I'm afraid of getting fired," which in turn might lead to "I'm afraid of failing to provide for my family." Now we're getting somewhere!) I keep digging deeper and deeper, trying to get to what I'm *really* afraid of. I will know it when it snatches my breath and I have a hard time saying it out loud.

5. I gather up the courage to say it out loud to God. And then I say it again and again until it gets a tiny bit easier to say. I speak with God about it and remain open to whatever God might say or do.

6. I ask God an important question: "Lord, is this fear realistic, or is it irrational?" For example, some people discover an unconscious fear of losing their job or having their spouse leave them, when all the while their conscious, rational self knows that there is practically no chance of this. If this is the case, I ask God for the ability to acknowledge the fear but not let it control my thoughts, words, or actions. On the other hand, if the fear is a reasonable one (I may actually get laid off soon), then I ask God, "What would you and I do then, Lord? How could we handle it?" If I listen carefully and with

peace in my heart, God will often intervene at this moment, consoling me by showing me how even this worst-case scenario will be manageable. God may even show me how growth and God's good will can emerge from such a difficult moment. Studies have shown that within six months most people recover from the most traumatic moments of their lives. And if this is true for the general population, how much more true must it be for those who have an intimate relationship with God!

7. Looking to tomorrow, I ask God for a particular *grace* or gift that will prevent this fear from getting the best of me. I pray for courage, fortitude, peace of mind and heart, trust in God, and acceptance of whatever comes.

8. I end in my usual way.

"Who do you say that I am?"

Once when Jesus was praying alone, with only the disciples near him, he asked them, "Who do the crowds say that I am?" They answered, "John the Baptist; but others, Elijah; and still others, that one of the ancient prophets has arisen." He said to them, "But who do you say that I am?" Peter answered, "The Messiah of God."

—Luke 9:18–20

1. I begin in my usual way.

2. I spend a few moments in gratitude, thanking God for one or two of the blessings, big and small, that I've received today.

3. I think about my relationship with God. I talk to God about how our relationship has been going lately. Are we getting along well? Do I feel close to or distant from God right now? Have I spent quality time with God or have I been neglectful? Do I sense that God is very close to me when I call on him? Am I bored with God? When I look upon the face of God, do I feel joy? gratitude? shame? fear? I speak with God about our relationship. I ask God to show me how he sees our relationship.

4. I read reflectively the Bible passage in which Jesus asks his disciples, "Who do you say that I am?" I quietly, peacefully watch the video in my mind of how today has

played out. As I watch each scene of my day, I ask myself, "Where was Christ in this moment? How did Christ come to me in this moment?"

5. After looking over a few of the details of my day, I back up now and look at the big picture. I ask myself, "Given all that's happened today, who was Christ for me today?" Was he:

- teacher?
- friend?
- consoler?
- coach?
- silent observer?
- spouse?
- savior?
- parent?

6. I say to Christ, "Lord, today you were _____ for me."

7. I now ask, "If you, Lord, were _____, then who am I in relationship to you?" I might say, "Lord, you were teacher and I was your student" or "Lord, you were my consoler and I was a brokenhearted soul in need of your healing." I speak to God awhile about the way our relationship played itself out today.

8. I now look to tomorrow. How do I want or need Christ to be present to me tomorrow? Do I need him to be my teacher? my friend? my savior? I tell Christ what it is I want or need from his presence in my life as I move forward.

9. I end in my usual way.

Choose Life

Surely, this commandment that I am commanding you today is not too hard for you, nor is it too far away. It is not in heaven, that you should say, "Who will go up to heaven for us, and get it for us so that we may hear it and observe it?" Neither is it beyond the sea, that you should say, "Who will cross to the other side of the sea for us, and get it for us so that we may hear it and observe it?" No, the word is very near to you; it is in your mouth and in your heart for you to observe.

See, I have set before you today life and prosperity, death and adversity. If you obey the commandments of the Lord your God that I am commanding you today, by loving the Lord your God, walking in his ways, and observing his commandments, decrees, and ordinances, then you shall live and become numerous, and the Lord your God will bless you in the land that you are entering to possess. But if your heart turns away and you do not hear, but are led astray to bow down to other gods and serve them, I declare to you today that you shall perish; you shall not live long in the land that you are crossing the Jordan to enter and possess. I call heaven and earth to witness against you today that I have set before you life and death, blessing and curses. Choose life so that you and your descendants may live.

—Deuteronomy 30:11–19

1. I begin in my usual way.

2. I spend a few moments in gratitude, thanking God for one or two of the blessings, big and small, that I've received today.

3. I slowly, prayerfully read the Bible passage above. Looking over my day, I ask myself, "Did I choose life or death today? Was the thrust of my life toward the good or toward the bad?" I do not analyze or dissect the parts of my day. Instead, I look at the overall movement of the day. Was it toward life or toward death? I speak with God about this. I give thanks and ask for forgiveness or for healing—whatever my heart feels inspired to say to God.

4. Now, I prayerfully imagine my day tomorrow, asking myself, "If I were to choose life tomorrow, what would my day look like? What would it *feel* like?" Perhaps I'll get concrete here and imagine specific things I will do or say that will mean life for me tomorrow (I'll be nice to the neighbor; I'll take a walk at the end of the day; I'll give my spouse a big kiss when I get home). Or perhaps I'll simply pray about my interior disposition (I'll choose to live out of peace rather than anger; I'll choose not to let my worries get the best of me). I speak with God about what it means to choose life tomorrow.

5. If I feel called to do so, I'll make a commitment to God, asking him to help me be faithful to that commitment.

6. I end in my usual way.

Examen 29

Places, Things, Activities

1. I begin in my usual way.

2. I spend a few moments in gratitude, thanking God for one or two of the blessings, big and small, that I've received today.

3. I review the **places** I've been today: home, workplace, the grocery store, a friend's apartment, the neighborhood park. Of all the places I've been today, for which am I most grateful? Which place makes it easy for me to be closer to God and more loving toward others? I thank God for this place and tell God how much it means to me.

4. Of all the places I've been today, which do I find to be a difficult place? Is there any place that is not healthy for me (a shopping mall, a bar)? Is there any place that I'm too attached to? I speak with God about this. I ask God for forgiveness, advice, and healing.

5. I review the material **things** in my life: car, phone, computer, clothes and accessories, food and drink. For which am I most grateful today? Which leads me closer to God and to my becoming a better Christian? I thank God for this blessing in my life.

6. Are any of these things keeping me from growing closer to God or others? Do any of these things lead me to sin? Am I too attached to any of them? Have I made a god of any of them? Is my ownership excessive, and am I being called to give something away and live more simply? I speak with God about this. I ask God for forgiveness, advice, and healing.

7. In the same way, I review the **activities** of my day: Going to work, eating, playing with the kids, exercising, watching TV, working hard at a task, sleeping, praying. For which am I most grateful? Which activities seem most "godly"? Which lead me closer to God and others? Which is a particularly good and healthy activity in my life? I speak with God about this, giving thanks.

8. Are any of my activities unhealthy, unholy, or unwholesome? Do any of my activities lead me away from faith, hope, and love? Do any lead me away from God? Am I addicted to any of these activities? I speak with God about this. I ask God for forgiveness, advice, and healing.

9. I now look back over this prayer time. What was the most enlightening or moving moment (regardless if it was enjoyable or painful)? What was my prayer at that moment? I go back to that moment and linger there, asking God if there is anything more he'd like to say or do in regard to this. Reflecting on this inspired moment, I ask God, "What, Lord, would you have me do tomorrow in regard to this place, thing, or activity?"

10. If appropriate, I make a commitment to God about this, and I ask for his help to keep this commitment.
11. I end in my usual way.

Examen 30

Persons

The Traditional Examen (Examen #1) has me praying over my day, moment by moment. Examen #29 has me prayerfully reviewing my day, not moment by moment, but rather place by place, thing by thing, activity by activity. This present Examen has me praying person by person, zooming in on the most important encounter of the day.

1. I begin in my usual way.

2. I spend a few moments in gratitude, thanking God for one or two of the blessings, big and small, that I've received today.

3. I ask God to show me each *person* I encountered today. I ask God to reveal which encounter today was the most important one. By "most important" I mean the conversation that had the strongest impact on me and/or the other person. It could be a negative or positive encounter. I zoom in on that one encounter.

    •   In that specific encounter, was I *spiritually free* or *unfree*? What led to my feeling spiritually free or unfree with this person? How does today's encounter relate to past encounters with this person? In general, am I spiritually free or unfree with this person? What leads to this spiritual freedom or unfreedom?

- What were the consequences of my spiritual freedom or unfreedom with this person? If I was free, what good came from it? I relish this good and praise God for it. If I was unfree, what bad came from it? I allow myself to feel the pain of this and ask God for forgiveness and healing.

4. Now I look to the future. When might I encounter this person again? What are my great *desires* for my relationship with this person? I allow my great desires to well up within me. I place these desires in God's hands and ask God to make them holy. I ask the Lord to show me what *grace* or virtue I need to be the person I want to be in this relationship. I ask for that grace or virtue.

5. If I feel called to do so, I make a resolution to be the kind of person I feel called to be in the relationships upon which I have reflected in this Examen.

6. I end in my usual way.

Where Are You? What Do You Seek?

*[Adam and Eve] heard the sound of the Lord God walking in
the garden at the time of the evening breeze, and the man and
his wife hid themselves from the presence of the Lord God
among the trees of the garden. But the Lord God called to the
man, and said to him, "Where are you?"*
—Genesis 3:8–9

*The two disciples heard [John the Baptist] say this, and they
followed him. When Jesus turned and saw them following, he
said to them, "What are you looking for?"*
—John 1:37–38

1. I begin in my usual way.

2. I spend a few moments in gratitude, thanking God for
    one or two of the blessings, big and small, that I've
    received today.

3. In my heart, I hear God asking me, *"Where are you?"* I sit
    with that question awhile before I even try to answer. I
    then begin by describing to God, as best I can, where I
    am today—mentally, physically, and most important,
    spiritually. I share with God my strongest thoughts and
    emotions. I try not to place judgments on those thoughts
    and emotions; I simply name them and turn them over
    to God.

4. Now, using *prayerful imagination*,

- I listen for anything the Lord might be trying to tell me at this moment. If I "hear" nothing, then I simply sit in God's presence as I present my response to his "Where are you?" question.
- I see Jesus' face before me, looking at me with love in his eyes. I hear him ask, *"What do you seek?"* I sit with that question awhile before I try to answer. I then begin to answer the Lord's question in a concrete way. I tell him about my great *desires* for myself, my family, my friends, my work, and so on.
- I listen for anything Jesus might be trying to tell me at this moment. If I "hear" nothing, then I simply sit in his presence as I present my response to his "What do you seek?" question.

5. I end in my usual way.

Examen 32

Past, Present, Future

1. I begin in my usual way.

2. I spend a few moments in gratitude, thanking God for one or two of the blessings, big and small, that I've received today.

3. I ask God to reveal to me my spiritual state of being this **past** day. What were my primary feelings throughout the day? Was I *spiritually free* or *unfree*? Or perhaps there were parts of the day wherein I was free and other parts wherein I was unfree? I ask God to show me the consequences of my spiritual freedoms and unfreedoms. I thank God for the good that came today. I ask for forgiveness and healing from any painful moments of the day.

4. I ask God to reveal to me my spiritual state at this **present** moment. What are my strongest thoughts and feelings at this very moment? I turn over these thoughts and feelings to God and ask God to make them holy. At this very moment, am I spiritually free or unfree? I give thanks or ask for healing.

5. I now look to the **future.** What attitudes and feelings am I likely to have tomorrow? Will it be a challenge to live in God's freedom tomorrow? If so, how and why will it be

challenging? What might be the most challenging moment? What *grace* or virtue (strength, fortitude, patience, courage, fidelity) might I need from God to live in his freedom? I ask God for that grace.

6. Now, perhaps the most important question: What would tomorrow be like if I were spiritually free all the day long? I allow myself to daydream such a wonderful day. I allow myself to experience great *desires* as I imagine myself moving through the day tomorrow. I ask God to show me the way to walk through this sort of day.

7. If I feel called to do so, I make a resolution to be the kind of person I feel called to be. I resolve, to the best of my ability, to live in freedom—in a realistic and particular way. I resolve to adopt one perspective over another one, to say these words instead of those, to do this thing rather than the other thing.

8. I end in my usual way.

Examen 33

The Hole in the Fortress Wall

Before his conversion, St. Ignatius fought in a battle defending the fortress of Pamplona, Spain. Later, after his conversion, he used that experience to talk about how the spirit of negativity within all of us tries to attack us at our weakest spots.

> [The spirit of negativity] conducts himself as a leader, intent upon conquering and robbing what he desires. For, just as a captain and leader of an army in the field, pitching his camp and exploring the fortifications and defenses of a stronghold, attacks it at the weakest point, in the same way the enemy of human nature, roving about, looks in turn at all our theological, cardinal, and moral virtues; and where he finds us weakest and most in need for our eternal salvation, there he attacks us and attempts to take us.
>
> —*The Spiritual Exercises*, #327

This Examen invites you to discover "the hole in your fortress wall."

1. I begin in my usual way.
2. I spend a few moments in gratitude, thanking God for one or two of the blessings, big and small, that I've received today.

3. Looking over the past day, I ask God to show me how a particular situation played into one of my weak spots. Which of my "buttons" was pushed today? What caused me to be oversensitive, prickly, overly emotional, neglectful, obtuse, or self-deceptive? At what moment did I:

   - react too strongly?
   - not react strongly enough (ignore/neglect)?
   - avoid an uncomfortable situation?
   - shirk my duties?
   - respond defensively, unkindly, crudely?
   - allow emotions to overwhelm me and get in the way?
   - refuse to acknowledge my emotions?

4. I may admit to God: "Lord, my sister really gets under my skin." "I noticed that I turn to food when I'm down." "Jealousy of my coworker led me to gossip about him." "I took my problems home today and snapped at my loved one." I say what I need to say. I ask for forgiveness and healing. I ask for healing of anyone I may have hurt because of this weak point in my spiritual life.

5. I now look to tomorrow and the days to come. I ask God to show me how this fortress hole affects me and others. What situations may try me in this sensitive area? I ask God to show me which virtues (strength? courage? humility? honesty? gentleness?) will help me shore up this sensitive area. I pray for that virtue now: "God, please grant me the _____ to deal with my own

problem with ____." I name the virtue repeatedly, asking God to grant it to me so that I might serve him better.

6. I end in my usual way.

Examen 34

Most Important Moments

1. I begin in my usual way.

2. I spend a few moments in gratitude, thanking God for one or two of the blessings, big and small, that I've received today.

3. I ask God to show me the *most important moment* of this day—the moment that had the biggest impact on me or on others, whether that impact be physical, spiritual, or emotional. Why was it so important? How was I feeling, deep down? Were there any negative thoughts or emotions that I did not admit to having (for example, fear of rejection)? Was I *spiritually free* or *unfree* in that most important moment? What were the consequences of that moment? As appropriate, I give thanks, I ask for forgiveness, I ask for healing.

4. If I wish and have the time to do so, I can return to my review of the day, asking God to show me another important moment of the day. I talk with God, using the same questions above. Again, I give thanks, ask for forgiveness, ask for healing.

5. Now, I look to tomorrow. Specifically, what do I think will be my most important moment tomorrow? What are my great *desires* for that moment? I allow my great

desires to well up within me. I place these desires in God's hands and ask God to make them holy. I ask God to show me what *grace* or virtue I need to be the person I want to be at that moment. I ask for that grace or virtue.

6. What other important moments may I experience tomorrow? I talk with God, using the reflection questions above.

7. If I feel called to do so, I make a concrete resolution to be the kind of person I feel called to be.

8. I end in my usual way.

Important Ignatian Terms

Desires

Here is one of St. Ignatius's most important insights: *God dwells in our greatest desires!* While many of the spiritual giants of Ignatius's day believed that a Christian is on the wrong path because she gives in to her desires, Ignatius had a different view: a Christian is on the wrong path because she is not in touch with her *truest* desires. God created the soul to desire great acts of faith, hope, and love. When it is not obstructed or distracted by sin, hurts, fears, or failures, the soul naturally moves toward faith, hope, and love. And even when the soul is bothered by negative movements, deeper down there will always be these great desires for being with God and for acting out of love. A key to the Christian life, then, is not to suppress my desires but to get in touch with the divine desires that dwell deep in my soul and are longing to burst out through my thoughts and actions.

In my Examen, I may explore the question: "What are my great desires right now?" By that I mean: Even in the midst of negativity, what does my better self long to do for God and for the world today? What acts of faith, hope, and love do I dream of doing?

Graces

The word *grace* is used in many different ways. In this book we are using it to mean "spiritual gift" or "virtue." I like to ask myself the question: "If I could ask God for one spiritual gift right now (courage, peace, clarity, patience, strength), what would it be?" Saint Ignatius believed that it is important to be aware of what he would call "the grace that you are seeking"—that is, of the spiritual gift or virtue you need or want at this moment. For example, if my coworker drove me crazy this morning, I might pray during my noontime Examen for the grace of patience. If I am hurt by something that a loved one said to me this morning, I might pray for the grace of patience or peace or temperance—whatever virtue I need to prevent my hurt feelings from leading me to think or act inappropriately. If I was tempted toward some particular sin this morning, I might pray for the grace of fortitude, of fidelity, of courage, of peace, or of spiritual discipline.

Praydreaming

Ignatius was a master daydreamer. He could do it for hours on end. It was through daydreaming that Ignatius learned to determine God's will for his life. He learned that God communicated God's will through great desires (see description above) for faith, hope, and love that welled up inside his heart and soul. By daydreaming in the context of prayer, Ignatius was able to allow those great desires to surface. Doing so would not only reveal God's will but also would fire him up to have the necessary passion to perform these great works.

In my own Examen, then, I praydream—prayerfully daydream. I concretely imagine how I might approach the next twenty-four hours if I were to be God's hands and feet and voice. I allow God to dream a dream within me of the wonderful ways I can be a channel of God's faith, hope, and love for the world. These praydreams give me the wisdom and the passion to carry out God's marvelous plans for me in the coming day.

Prayerful Imagination

Cynics and skeptics of prayer say that those who pray don't really hear God's voice or see God's face. They say instead that it is "just their imagination." People who pray often take up the argument with something like, "No, it's *not* my imagination, it really is God speaking to me!" But we who pray should reject the whole premise of the cynic's argument because it presumes that God can't speak to me *through* my imagination. God is the inventor and creator of the gift of the imagination, and he loves what he has created! Of course, God will speak to me and appear to me in my imagination, provided I allow God to do so.

I use the phrase *prayerful imagination* to indicate that I allow God to come to me through my imagination. For example, if, in my heart of hearts, I deeply desire for Christ to answer some question of mine, then I imagine Christ sitting beside me. I look right at him and he looks right at me, and in my imagination he speaks to me.

But isn't it possible that I put words in Christ's mouth? Might I get him to say in my imagination exactly what I would want him to say? Yes, that is possible. For this reason, I don't take anything I learn in prayer at face value. Instead, I return to it in prayer, I ponder it as I journal about my prayer, I discuss it with a wise friend and/or a spiritual director. In the end, I trust that

God desires to speak to me and will do so in whatever way I allow him to. Through persistence in prayer and in pondering the meaning of my prayer, God himself will help me sort out his own words and actions from the stuff that doesn't come from him. Because I believe so strongly in God's desire to communicate with me and I trust in his ability to keep me from deceiving myself, I respectfully choose to ignore the cynics and let my imagination run wild and free in my prayer. God and I will make great use of it as we grow closer in intimate companionship.

Spiritual Freedom and Unfreedom

I am spiritually free when my spiritual and emotional state of being is healthy. I am spiritually free when I am emotionally well-balanced and when I desire to be a faithful, hopeful, and loving person. I am spiritually unfree when my negative emotions and temptations have gotten the better of me, when I am too angry, sad, tempted, or scared to think straight. I am unfree when I am lethargic and not inspired to be more faithful, hopeful, and loving. I am unfree when I don't feel God's presence at this moment and I don't care or am too panicky to handle the situation well.

So, in my Examen, I may explore the question: "What was my most unfree moment this morning?" By that I mean: When precisely was I in a bad mood? The moment that the unfaithful, unhopeful, unloving side of me took over? The moment when I let my strong negative emotions control my thoughts and actions?

I might then explore the question: "What was my most free moment?" By that I mean: When precisely was I in a really good mood? The moment that the most faithful, hopeful, and loving side of me was running the show? The moment when I was thinking clearly and objectively and was thinking good and loving thoughts and making good and loving decisions?

A Note of Thanks

I am overwhelmed with gratitude for all the people who have supported me, particularly in my vocation to write. Thank you to my unconditionally loving family: Mom, Dad, Steve, Cameron, Demi, Brianna, Greg, Nancy, Ashley, Dillon, Stuart, Stacey, Abbie, Michael, Eric, Sandy, Marty, and Coy.

Thank you to my other unconditionally loving family: my brother Jesuits. I am unworthy of your company.

Thanks to Tucker Redding, Anthony Ostini, Jim Goeke, and all those who provided assistance and advice throughout my writing of this book.

Thanks especially to those whom I've had the privilege of guiding through the novitiate. Be careful out there: remember what people do all the time. You, my former novices, both those who ended up SJs and those who didn't, have been some of the greatest gifts of my life.

A special thank-you to Christopher Kellerman, SJ, for being my loving-but-tough editorial sparring partner. This book is infinitely better because of your tireless work, your sharp eye, and your patient kindness. You are a good friend and a gifted writer. I can't wait to see your first book in print!

I dedicate this book to the memory of Annette Harris Thibodeaux, the first of our generation to make it to heaven. We love you and miss you, Annette. May you have an eternity of delightful friends, strong coffee, and good wine.

About the Author

Mark E. Thibodeaux, SJ, serves as novice director for Jesuits in formation and is an acknowledged expert on the topic of prayer and discernment. He is a well-known speaker and the author of *God, I Have Issues*, *Armchair Mystic*, and *God's Voice Within*. He lives in Grand Coteau, Louisiana.

Notes

Notes

Notes

Notes

Also Available

God's Voice Within
$14.95 | 2861-2 | PB

A Simple, Life-Changing Prayer
$9.95 | 3535-1 | PB

God Finds Us
$9.95 | 3827-7 | PB

The Ignatian Adventure
$14.95 | 3577-1 | PB

TO ORDER, call 800.621.1008, visit **www.loyolapress.com**
or visit your local bookseller.

Ignatian Spirituality Online
www.ignatianspirituality.com

Visit us online to

- Join our *E-Magis* newsletter

- Pray the Daily Examen

- Make an online retreat with the *Ignatian Prayer Adventure*

- Participate in the conversation with the dotMagis blog and at **facebook.com/ignatianspirituality**